Amazing Cars For Kids: A Children's Picture Book About Cars

A Great Simple Picture Book for Kids to Learn about Different Cars

Melissa Ackerman

PUBLISHED BY:

Melissa Ackerman

Disclaimer

The information contained in this book is for general information purposes only. The information is provided by the authors and while we endeavor to keep the information up to date and correct, we make no representations or warranties of any kind, express or implied, about the completeness, accuracy, reliability, suitability or availability with respect to the book or the information, products, services, or related graphics contained in the book for any purpose. Any reliance you place on such information is therefore strictly at your own risk.

TABLE OF CONTENTS

AC Cobra

AC Cobra is a British sports car known in the US as the Shelby Cobra. They are also sold in the United States as Shelby AC Cobra. It was produced from 1962 to 1967. It is one of the most famous and frequently imitated cars on the road. Indeed, AC Cobra is an instant classic hit.

Alfa Romeo 33 Stradale

Alfa Romeo 33 Stradale is an Italian sports car built by Alfa Romeo between 1967 and 1969. Throughout its entire 2-year production life, only 18 Stradale were made. Its curvaceous body is truly an eye-catcher. Stradale is the Italian word for "road-going".

Alfa Romeo 8C Competizione

Alfa Romeo 8C Competizione is an Italian sports car produced from 2007 to 2010 by Alfa Romeo. After its official announcement of the car's production, Alfa Romeo received over 1,400 orders of 8C. Only 500 customers were given *C Competizione. Another 500 received 8C Spider, an open car version of the Competizione.

Alfa Romeo Spider

Alfa Romeo Spider is a two-seater convertible car. It was built by the Italian manufacturer Alfa Romeo from 1966 up to 1993. The name spider comes from the English word "speeder", a two-seater open horse carriage. Though the Spider has several variants, the original "Series 1" become famous and was featured in the movie *The Graduate*.

Aston Martin DB4

Aston Martin DB4 is a sports car sold by Aston Martin from 1958 to 1963. Throughout its production lifetime, there were a total of 1,210 DB4 units produced. It also has a lightweight body designed in Milan by Carrozzeria Touring. Its stunning look leaves a positive impression at the 1958 London Motor Show.

Aston Martin DB5

Aston Martin DB5 is a British luxury car produced between 1963 and 1965. In total, there were 1,023 units built. It was also made by Aston Martin but the design was by Carrozzeria Touring Superleggera, an Italian coachbuilder. DB5 is famous for appearing in Goldfinger, a James Bond series.

Aston Martin DB6

Aston Martin DB6 is a British car produced by Aston Martin. It was manufactured from 1965 to 1971. This particular car also has three variants, the DB6 Mark II (with wider wheels), DB6 Vantage (high-powered type) and Volante (convertible style). Though it's not as gorgeous as the Aston Martin's previous model DB5, it's still pretty and has some advanced development in its technical aspect.

Aston Martin DB9

Aston Martin DB9 was first launched by Aston Martin at the Frankfurt Motor Show in 2003. It was offered both in a hardtop and in a convertibles style known as the Volante. It's production run from 2004 to 2016. The DB on its name is the initials of David Brown, the owner of Aston Martin.

Aston Martin One-77

Aston Martin One-77 is a two-door hardtop British car. It was built by Aston Martin from 2009 to 2012. The number of car produced was limited to 77 cars. So if you own one you are one of the 77 that owns the One-77. It has a jaw-dropping price tag of almost $2 million. To date, it has the company's largest and most powerful engine.

Audi R8

Audi R8 is a high performance very expensive sports car built from 2006 up to present. It was produced by the German automaker Audi AG. It is also the first car built with full-LED headlamps. Audi R8 was adored universally because of its powerful engine and unique appearance.

Audi S6

Audi S6 is a high performance variant of the Audi A6, an executive car. An executive car is a car larger than a mid-sized car. Its production started in 1994. The latest generation of S6 is one of the best-looking sedans ever made with its modern, tightly sculpted and luxury design style.

Austin-Healey 100

Austin-Healey 100 is a sports car by Austin-Healey which was produced from 1953 until 1956. In 1952, Healey built one Healey Hundred for the London Motor Show. The design impressed Leonard Lord, the managing director of the motor vehicle company called Austin. They had a deal and the car was built in quantity with bodies made by Jensen Motors. It was also renamed from Healey Hundred to Austin-Healey 100. The 100 from its name was because this car could hit 100 mph.

Austin-Healey 3000

Austin-Healey 3000 is a British sports car. It was built from 1959 to 1967. The vehicle was assembled by Austin-Healey, but Jensen Motors is the one who made the car's bodywork. It is also the best known out of the "Big Healey" models (big Austin-Healey cars which includes Austin-Healey 100, Austin-Healey 100-6 and Austin-Healey 300).

Auto Union Type C

Auto Union Type C is the third evolution of Auto Union's race car. All in all, there were Auto Union Type A, Auto Union Type B, Auto Union Type C and Auto Union Type D. The Type C in particular is one of history's most highly regarded race cars. It competed with Mercedes-Benz and also raced against other amazing sports cars. In 1936, Type Cs won six victories and made Bernt Rosermeyer the world champion.

BMW 3.0 CSL

The BMW 3.0CSL is a variation of the BMW E9. It was produced between 1972 and 1975. It was specifically built to be eligible for racing at the European Touring Car Championship. It was specially made lighter compared to other BMW models. It was also considered as one of the rarest and most beloved BMW car of all time.

BMW 507

The BMW 507 is an open car built by BMW from 1956 to 1959. Originally, it was intended to be exported in the United Stated at a rate of thousands per year. But it ended up as being too expensive, only 252 cars were produced. It also results to heavy losses for BMW.

BMW M1

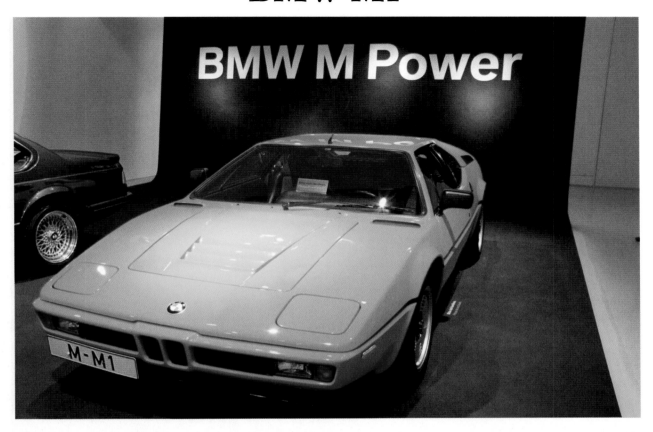

The BMW M1 is a sports car manufactured from 1978 to 1981. It is one of the rarest BMW models and is specially designed for car racing. In the 1970s, Lamborghini and BMW entered an agreement to build a production racing car. Conflicts arose and BMW was prompted to build the car themselves. The result was mass-produced and was sold to the public as BMW M1.

BMW M6

BMW M6 is a high performance version of the BMW 6 Series. It was designed by the motorsport division of BMW and was produced 1983 – 1989, 2005 – 2010, and 2012 – present. The original M6 was admired for its elegant and aggressive styling. Its front part is shaped like a shark's nose.

BMW Z8

BMW Z8 is a convertible car manufactured by BMW from 1999 to 2003. Its cost was around $128,000. Z8 was eventually BMW's answer to growing demand for a high end convertible.

Bugatti Type 57

The Bugatti Type 57 is a big hit shortly before World War II. It is built from 1934 – 1940. It was a new design and only 710 units were produced. It also has two variants, the Type 57 and the Type 57s. The Type 57 is the original version. The Type 57s on the other hand is the lowered version of Type 57.

Bugatti Veyron

Bugatti Veyron is a sports car designed and developed in Germany by the Volkswagen Group. But it was manufactured in France by the Bugatti Automobiles S.A.S. Its production ran from 2005 to 2015. Its original version received a best car award and was named as the Car of the Decade (2000 – 2009) by Top Gear, a British television series about motor vehicles. For the record, Bugatti Veyron hits the speed of nearly 268 miles per hour.

Cadillac (1959)

The 1959 Cadillac is also referred to as Cadillac Eldorado, a personal luxury car manufactured from 1953 – 2002. The original 1953 Eldorado convertible and the Eldorado Brougham models of 1957 – 1960 were the most expensive car models from Cadillac during those years. In line with the celebration of the company's golden anniversary, this model was named Eldorado. This name was derived from El Dorado, a mythical South American "Lost City of Gold".

Chevrolet Camaro

Chevrolet Camaro is a car manufactured by Chevrolet. It is classified as a pony car (an American automobile inspired by Ford Mustang) Pony cars are less expensive and compact. Some of its later versions are designed to be a muscle car too (an American automobile capable of high-performance driving). It is a classic car designed to compete with Ford Mustang. The production of Chevrolet Camaro ended in 2002.

Chevrolet Corvette

The first generation of Chevrolet Corvette was introduced in 1953. The production lasts up until 1962. It was originally designed as a car show to be displayed at the New York Auto Show. Many people have shown interest with the car. So, on June 30, 1953, a production version was made and sold to the public. It was considered as the most significant American car. Its impressive performance and stylish design proved that America could compete with other sports car manufacturers.

Chevrolet Corvette (C2)

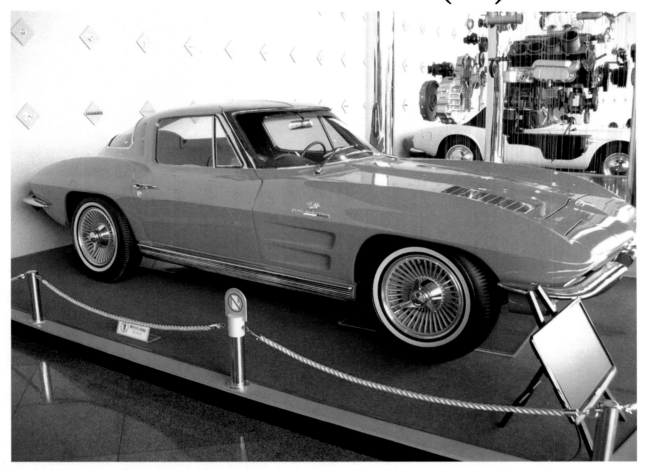

Chevrolet Corvette (C2) is also known as the Corvette Sting Ray. This sports car was produced from 1963 to 1967. Its rear view window whish was split into two is very unique and was instantly recognizable.

Dodge Viper SRT

The Dodge Viper SRT or SRT Viper is a sports car manufactured by Chrysler. The production starts in 1992 and is about to end when the CEO announced and showed in 2010 the new model of the Viper for 2012. It has then become famous not only because of its macho-like appearance but also because it can run super-fast.

Duesenberg Model J

Duesenberg Model J is a luxury automobile produced by Duesenberg from 1928 to 1937. It is specifically built to compete with the most luxurious and most powerful cars in the world including Mercedes-Benz and Rolls-Royce. It also holds the crown as the most powerful prewar American vehicle.

Ferrari 250 GTO

Ferrari 250 GTO is a racing car from Ferrari manufactured from 1962 – 1964. In 2012, the 1962 250 GTO made for Stirling Moss (a British F1 racing driver) is the world's most expensive car in history. It was sold for $38,115,000 to Craig McRaw, an American businessman.

Ferrari 275

Ferrari 275 was manufactured by Ferrari between 1964 and 1968. Pininfarina from Italy was the one who designed its body. This handsome car was the last car model produced before Ferrari evolved into a more angular design style.

Ferrari 288 GTO

Ferrari 288 GTO is also known as Ferrari GTO. It was built from 1984 through 1987 and was the fastest car ever made at the time. It was specifically built to compete at the new Group B Race series or a race competition for the fastest and most powerful car ever made. After the death of a driver and a co-driver in a 1986 race, Class B Race was disestablished. As a result, 288 GTO never raced and all the 272 units built remained as purely road cars.

Ferrari 330 P4

Ferrari 330 P4 is a legendary racing car used only for the highest level categories of sports car racing. There were only three 330 P4 cars produced. Because of its fame, more than a hundred of P4 replicas have been built.

Ferrari 360 Modena

Ferrari 360 is a two-seater sports car produced by Ferrari from 1999 to 2005. The 360 Modena was the first model to be shipped. It was named after the town of Modena, the birthplace of Enzo Ferrari founder of Ferrari. With its eye catching look, the 360 Modena has been Ferrari's bread and butter sports car during that time.

Ferrari 458 Italia

Ferrari 458 Italia is an Italian sports car that replaced the Ferrari F430. It was officially launched at the 2009 Frankfurt Motor Show. In line with its tradition, the body of the 458 Italia was designed by Pininfarina, an Italian car design firm and coachbuilder. Aside from its stunning looks, 458 Italia can perform seriously on the racetrack.

Ferrari 550 Maranello

Ferrari 550 Maranello is a two-seater grand tourer (GT), an automobile capable of high-performance distance driving. It was produced between 1996 and 2001. The name Maranello was named after the town of Maranello, the home of Ferrari's headquarters and factory.

Ferrari 599 GTB Fiorano

The Ferrari 599 GTB Fiorano is an Italian sports car produced from 2006 to 2012. It replaced the 575M Maranello. This stunning car is also one of Ferrari's fastest automobile ever built.

Ferrari Dino

Ferrari Dino was produced by Ferrari from 1968 to 1976. It was Ferrari's attempt to offer a low-cost sports car that is capable of taking on the Porsche 911. Its name was to honor Enzo Ferrari's son and heir, Dino Ferrari.

Ferrari Enzo

Ferrari Enzo is a sporty type two-door closed car. It is a high performance and very expensive model. It was manufactured from 2002 until 2004 with a limited production run of 399. It was also named after Ferrari's founder, Enzo Ferrari. Before being unveiled at the Paris Motor Show, the Enzo was flown to California to be filmed in Charlie's Angels: Full Throttle. It was driven on a beach by actress Demi Moore. In 2004, the 400th Enzo was built and donated to the Vatican for charity.

Ferrari F40

Ferrari F40 is a sports car built from 1987 to 1992. It was designed in line with the celebration of Ferrari's 40th anniversary. It was also the last Ferrari model that was personally approved by Enzo Ferrari. At the time, Ferrari F40 was the most expensive, most powerful and the fastest car sold by Ferrari. During its production life, 1,311 units were produced.

Ferrari F430

Ferrari F430 is an Italian sports car produced by the car manufacturer Ferrari. It was built from 2004 to 2009. It has a more athletic look compared to the previous 360 Modena. In 2009, Ferrari recalled about 2,000 units of the 2005 – 2007 models F430 Spiders in the US due to some mechanical issues that may cause fire.

Ferrari F50

Ferrari F50 is a sports car introduced from 1995 to 1997. Throughout its production lifetime, only 349 cars were built. It is a two-door and two-seater car with a removable hardtop. Compared to F40, the F50 is more curvaceous and is exotically beautiful. A custom-made F50 variant named the Bolide was ordered by the Sultan of Brunei in 1998.

Ferrari Testarossa

Ferrari Testarossa is another sports car manufactured by Ferrari. Its production life lasts from 1984 to 1996. With 10,000 units produced, Testarossa is one of the most produced Ferrari models despite its high price and exotic unmistakable look.

Ford Boss 302 Mustang

The Ford Boss 302 Mustang is a variant of the Ford Mustang. It is a high performance automobile manufactured to compete with Chevrolet Camaro. It is originally produced in 1969 and 1970. In 2012 and 2013, Ford revived the model and produced it for the Trans Am Racing series (a series of road races for sports car).

Ford GT40

Ford GT40 is a high performance British-American racing car. It was manufactured from 1964 to 1969. It won the 24 Hours of Lemans (a French sports car race) four times from 1966 to 1969. It was originally produced to compete and win against Ferrari (a champion in Le Mans) in a long-distance sports car races. It indeed beats Ferrari and is the only American car to win the great French race.

Ford Thunderbird

Ford Thunderbird is an automobile manufactured in the United States by Ford. From 1995 to 2005, the Thunderbird has eleven model generations. It was also not marketed as a sports car. Instead, it was marketed as a personal luxury car. Indeed, Ford Thunderbird is a true classic car.

Honda NSX

Honda NSX is a sports car marketed in North America as the Acura NSX. Its production ran from 1990 to 2005. It was then reproduced last 2015 until today. NSX stands for "New", "Sportscar", "Experimental". It was designed to compete and exceed Ferrari cars' performance with a lower price point.

Honda S2000

Honda S2000 is an open or convertible car manufactured in Japan from 1999 to 2009. The launching of this car was part of Honda's 50th anniversary celebration. It also has two official variants, the AP1 and the AP2 or AP1 Facelift. The AP2 is a bit bigger than the AP1.

Hudson Hornet

Hudson Hornet is an automobile manufactured by the Hudson Motor Car Company of Detroit, Michigan. Its production life was from 1952 to 1954. It was also later produced by the American Motors Corporation in Kenosha, Wisconsin between 1955 and 1957. It has a very unique lower and sleeker appearance.

Jaguar C-Type

The Jaguar C-Type is also called as the Jaguar XK120-C. It is a lightweight racing sports car sold from 1951 to 1953. The "C" on its name stands for competition. The C-Type is successful when it comes to racing. It actually won twice at the Le Mans 24 hours race, the world's oldest active sports car race.

Jaguar E-Type

Jaguar E-Type is also known as the Jaguar XK-E. It was manufactured by Jaguar Cars, Ltd from 1961 to 1975. It has become an icon in the 1960s because of its beauty, high performance and competitive price. In 2004, it was number one on the list of Sports Car International magazine's *Top Sports Cars of the 1960s*.

Jaguar XJ13

Jaguar XJ13 is a racing car produce by Jaguar for the 24 Hours of Le Mans in 1966. However, it never raced and only one unit was made. For the launching film of KJ13, they wanted a shot of the car while it is running. Unfortunately, the car crashed and the XJ13 was nearly destroyed. The driver was unharmed but the wrecked car was put back into the storage.

Jaguar XJS

Jaguar XJS is the one that replaced the Jaguar E-type. It is a luxurious automobile for high-speed long distance driving. It is also a great looking car and is by far one of the most recognizable models from Jaguar. For 21 years, there are a total of 115,413 units produced.

Jaguar XK

The Jaguar XK is a series of luxury automobiles capable of high-speed distance driving. It was produced in 1996 and was first introduced at the Geneva Motor Show. The last car of this particular model came off the production line on 23 July 2014. Compared to previously built XK cars, the latest generation of Jaguar XK screams modern elegance.

Jaguar XK120

The Jaguar XK120, a postwar British car was manufactured between 1948 and 1954. It was Jaguar's first sports car since the SS 100. It was first launched as a show car at the 1948 London Motor Show. Many showed interest to the car persuading the Jaguar founder to produce more units and put it on sale.

Jaguar XKSS

The Jaguar XKSS is a road-going version of the Jaguar D-Type racing car. Because Jaguar has withdrew from entering racing competitions in 1956, there were some D-Types that remained unsold. To recover some of the investments, some of the D-Types were converted to road-going cars. The actor Steve McQueen owned a Jaguar XKSS and he called it the "Green Rat".

Koenigsegg Agera

The Koenigsegg Agera is a sports car produced between 2011 and 2014 by the Swedish company Koenigsegg. Its name comes from the Swedish verb "agera" meaning "to act". It was also named "Hypercar of the Year" in 2010 by Top Gear Magazine, an automobile magazine. This particular car model takes performance to a nearly unbelievable level with its 270 miles per hour top speed.

Lamborghini Aventador

Lamborghini Aventador was first launched in 2011 at the Geneva Motor Show. It was designed to replace Lamborghini's ten-year old Murcielago as the new model. Soon after its unveiling, 12 Aventador units were already sold. By 2013, Lamborghini had already built 2,000 Aventadors. In line with the company's naming tradition, the bull which the Aventador was named after earned a trophy for its courage in the arena.

Lamborghini Diablo

Lamborghini Diablo is a high performance sports car. It was built by Italian automaker Lamborghini from 1990 to 2001. It was the first Lamborghini model that attains the top speed exceeding 200 miles per hour. Lamborghini has a tradition of naming its cars after breeds of fighting bulls. Diablo was a ferocious bull raised in the 19th century. It is believed that Lamborghini Diablo was designed to become the biggest head-turner in the world.

Lamborghini Gallardo

Lamborghini Gallardo is a sports car manufactured from 2003 to 2013. It is Lamborghini's best-selling model with 14,022 units produced throughout its production. With its strikingly unique design, Gallardo is destined to compete with Ferrari sports cars. Like other Lamborghini models, Gallardo was named after a famous breed of a fighting bull.

Lamborghini Miura

Lamorghini Miura is an Italian high performance sports car created by Lamborghini from 1966 to 1973. When released, it became the fastest road car available. It was also made to compete against and dethrone Ferrari.

Lamborghini Murcielago

Lamborghini Murcielago is an Italian sports car produced from 2001 to 2010. There are a total of 4,099 cars built throughout its entire production life. It was also Lamborghini's first model under the ownership of Audi, which is owned by Volkswagen. An open car version of the Murcielago was introduced in 2004.

Lamborghini Reventon

Lamborghini Reventon is a sports car launched at the Frankfurt Motor Show in 2007. It was one of the most expensive Lamborghini road cars costing $2 million. There are only 21 Reventon produced. Twenty were to be sold to the public while the last one was for the Lamborghini museum. Its exterior styling was inspired by "the fastest airplanes".

Lexus LFA

Lexus LFA is a two-seater supercar or very expensive and high performance sports car. The production of this particular car starts in 2010 and ended in 2012. Throughout its 2-year production life, 500 LFA units were completed.

Lincoln Continental

Lincoln Continental is a luxury car marketed by Lincoln, a division of Ford Motor Company. It was first introduced in 1939 and is still being produced until today. Now, in order to produce fuel-efficient vehicles, the Continental was changed from being a full-size to a mid-size. The 1965 model year was the favorite of car enthusiasts.

Lotus Elite

Lotus Elite was manufactured from 1958 to 1963. Its name has been used for three vehicles from Lotus cars. These car models are the Type 14, Types 75 & 83 and the 2014 Elite. Additionally, the original Elite is extremely lightweight.

Lotus Elise

Lotus Elise is a two-seater convertible car. It's tiny, lightweight and fast. It was released in 1996 by the British manufacturer Lotus Cars. The name Elise originates from Elisa, the granddaughter of Romano Artioli who was the chairman of Lotus and Bugatti at the time of the car's launch.

Lotus Esprit

Lotus Esprit is a sports car built by Lotus. It is manufactured in the United Kingdom up to 2004. The name Kiwi was originally proposed for this model. But, in order to keep the Lotus tradition of having all the name of car models start with the letter "E", the name becomes Esprit. The 1993-2004 models or the so called S4 variant is the result of a major exterior and interior redesign of the earlier Lotus Esprit versions. It also became the peak of popularity of this particular model.

Lotus Evora

Lotus Evora is a British sports car from Lotus. It was manufactured from 2009 up to present. It was developed under the project name "Project Eagle". It has larger interior that allows taller people to fit inside. It is also the answer for those who are looking for a more practical alternative to the tiny Lotus Elise. The name Evora was derived from the words evolution, vogue and aura.

Maserati 3500 GT

The Maserati 3500 GT is an Italian car manufactured by Maserati between the years 1957 and 1964. During the start of the car's production in 1957, there were a total of 18 units built. It was also Maserati's breakthrough into the GT (grand tourer) market or automobiles capable of long distance high-speed journeys.

Mazda RX7

Mazda RX7 is a Japanese sports car manufactured between 1978 and 2002 by Mazda. It has a hardtop and pop-up headlamps. It is a two-seater sports car but buyers can have a back seat installed for them. RX7 has also become popular through The Fast and the Furious series: Initial D. Need for Speed, Wangan Midnight, Forza Motorsport and Gran Turismo,

McLaren F1

McLaren F1 is a supercar or high performance very expensive car manufactured by McLaren Cars. It was built from 1992 to 1999. In 1998, it set the record as the world's fastest car, hitting 231 miles per hour. It is possibly the best sports car ever made.

McLaren MP4-12C

McLaren MP4-12C is later known simply as the McLaren 12C. It is a high performance sports car designed and manufactured by McLaren Automotive from 2011 to 2014. A convertible version of McLaren 12C was also available and released in 2012. It was called the MP4-12C Spider and renamed 12C Spider.

Mercedes-Benz 300SL

The Mercedes-Benz 300SL was introduced in 1954. Its production ended in 1963. It was notable for its unique gull-wing doors. With these doors, 300SL immediately become successful and was today an iconic car. It was also the world's fastest car at the time.

Mercedes-Benz 540K

The Mercedes-Benz 540 was manufactured by Mercedes-Benz from 1935 – 1940. It is one of the largest cars of the time. It is also available in two seater, four seater and seven seater variants. With such a distinctive style, the 540K has remarkable sleeker and curvier bodywork.

Mercedes-Benz SLS AMG

Mercedes-Benz SLS AMG is a luxurious limited production high performance car developed by Mercedes-AMG of Mercedes-Benz. It also had gull-wing doors. The SLS stands for "Sport Leicht Super", German for Sport Light Super. In 2011 an electric version of the car called the SLS AMG Electric Drive was presented in the United States.

Mercedes-Benz SSK

Mercerdes-Benz SSK is a German open car built between 1928 and 1932. Its name is the abbreviation of Super Sport Kurz, German for "Super Sport Short". Because of its extreme performance, it became one of the most highly regarded sports cars during that time. Today, it is the most sought after cars in the world. This is because there are only four or five entirely original models remaining.

Mercury Coupe

Mercury Coupe is the third generation or evolution of Mercury Eight, a full-sized automobile. It was manufactured from 1949 to 1951 by Mercury, the American-market division of Ford Motor Company. Since it was launched in 1949, it has become famous and immediately became the ride of choice for customizers.

MG MGA

MGA is a sports car introduced by MG. It was manufactured from 1955 to 1962. It was officially launched at the Frankfurt Motor Show. With its modern, attractive and lightweight design, this particular car model is truly successful. Until the end of its production, there were a total of 101,081MGA units sold.

Morgan Plus 4

The Morgan Plus 4 is an automobile built by the Morgan Motor Company. It was produced from 1950 to 1969. It was then revived in 1985 until 2000. And in 2005, it was again reproduced up until today. With its traditional style combined with modern concepts, Plus 4 indeed is an attractive English car.

Nissan Fairlady Z

The Nissan Fairlady Z or Nissan S30 is also known as the Datsun 240Z, then later as 260Z and 280Z. It was the first generation of Nissan Z-car, a series of sports car manufactured by Nissan Motors, Ltd. of Japan. The Nissan Fairlady Z was produced 1969 – 1978. It was also considered as the most important car in Japan's history because it proved that the country could compete in the worldwide auto market.

Nissan GT-R

The Nissan GT-R was first launched in 2007 at the Tokyo Motor Show. Seven months later, this particular model was launched in the United States and in Canada. Indeed, this car got the looks and it uses high technology and yet, Nissan GTR does not cost as much as the other exotic supercars. Up until today, Nissan GT-R is still being produced.

Noble M400

Noble M400 is a British sports car manufactured by Noble Automotive Ltd from 2004 – 2007. To date, Noble no longer manufactures the M400. The production rights to M400 was obtained by 1G Racing (Rossion) in Ohio, USA. 1G Racing released an updated version of M400 named Rossion Q1.

Pagani Zonda

Pagani Zonda is an Italian sports car built by Pagani. It was built from 1999 to 2011. It has three specials edition cars. These are the Zonda 760RS, Zonda 760LH and the Zonda 764 Passione. This particular car was originally named the "Fangio F1" after Juan Manuel Fangio, who engineered the early Zonda. After his death in 1995, it was renamed Zonda, a term for an air current above Argentina.

Pontiac Firebird

Pontiac Firebird is an automobile built from 1967 to 2002. It was introduced in the same year as with Chevrolet Corvette. It has also become famous for its role in the show *Smokey and the Bandit*. The large bird painted on its hood is one of its remarkable features.

Porsche 356

Porsche 356 is a luxury sports car introduced by the Austrian company Porsche Konstruktionen GesmbH from 1948 to 1949. It was Porsche's first automobile. It was also created by Ferdinand Porsche, co-founder of the Austrian company. He was also the one who designed the Volkswagen Beetle.Porsche 356 is lightweight and a quite popular car in the motorsports world.

Porsche 550

The Porsche 550 was a racing sports car built by Porsche in 1953 to 1956. It was designed very low to the ground in order to be competent in racing. 550 won its first race in May 1953. The racer James Dean who owned a 550 used it and died in an accident during a race.

Porsche 959

Porsche 959 is a sports car sold from 1986 to 1989. During its launching, 959 was the "world's fastest street-legal production car". During its production, it was also considered as the most technologically advanced road-going sports car ever built. 959 is truly an automotive icon of the 80s.

Ruf CTR

The Ruf CTR was a heavily modified Porsche 911 also known as the CTR Yellowbird or simply Yellowbird. It was a high performance sports car built by Ruf Automobile. It was also limited in production with only 29 units built from scratch. The rest were just conversions from customer's existing cars.

SS Cars SS100

SS Cars SS100 was later known as SS Jaguar 100. It is a British two-seater sports car built between 1936 and 1940 by SS Cars Ltd. in Coventry, England. Just like any other products of the 30s, the adoption of an animal name was deemed appropriate. Once approved by Sir William Lyons, the name Jaguar was given to the new car and to all upcoming cars. In 1945, after the World War II, the company was renamed from SS Cars Ltd to Jaguar.

Talbot-Lago T150 CSS

Talbot-Lago T150 CSS is also known as the teardrop. It was a successful racing car from the 30s. The T150 CSS has considerable racing competition success. It also features a jaw-dropping amazing sleek design.

Toyota 2000GT

The Toyota 2000GT is a limited-production hardtop car designed by Toyota in partnership with Yamaha. It was manufactured under contract by Yamaha from 1967 to 1970. Today, this car model is seen as the first seriously collectible car. A convertible version of 2000GT was also used in a James Bond film *You Only Live Twice*.

Triumph GT6

Triumph GT6 is a sports car built by Standard-Triumph. Its production ran from 1966 to 1972. It was also built based from the popular Triumph Spitfire. Though the company was best known for their traditional convertible cars, the new GT6 was produced with a permanent hardtop.

Triumph Spitfire

Triumph Spitfire is an English sports car introduced in 1962 at the London Motor Show. It was a convertible car but factory-made hard tops were also available. Officially, there are five Triumph Spitfire models sold during its production run (1962 – 1980).

Triumph TR6

Triumph TR6 is a British sports car built by Triumph. Though it is slightly old-fashioned in design, it is still one of the most beloved in England's convertible. It is also the best-seller amongst the Triumph TR range of cars when the production ended in July 1976. In total, there are 94,619 TR6 produced.

TVR Griffith

TVR Griffith is a sports car built and designed by TVR. It represents a new era that brings the makers of this car back to the spotlight by its stylish curvaceous design. The production of this specific car model starts is in 1991 and ended in 2002. And to mark the end of production, TVR manufactured 100 Special Edition Griffith cars.

TVR Griffith 200

The TVR Griffith 200 or Griffith Series 200 is a lightweight sports car. This car model is frighteningly fast with its 150 miles per hour top speed. The concept with the Griffith Series 200 originated over a dinner when Jack Griffith, a car repair workshop owner said he could build a car that could outperform the AC Cobra.

TVR Tuscan

The TVR Tuscan is a sports car built in Blackpool, England from 1967 to 1971. With only 174 units made throughout is production life, Tuscan is a rare sight even on British roads. It is also available in two formats or engine types, the V6 and the V8. The V6 model is narrower than the V8 model.

TVR Tuscan Speed Six

TVR Tuscan Speed Six is a sports car manufactured in the United Kingdom by TVR between 1999 and 2006. TVR surprisingly rejects the notion that "airbags" is a safety device. They believe that based on experience and testing, their cars safer without this than with them. With its "spidery eyes" and stylish shape, TVR Tuscan Speed Six is truly a sight on the road.

Volkswagen Karmann Ghia

Volkswagen Karmann Ghia is a sports car marketed by Volkswagen in 1955-1974. It was built from the existing Beetle model featuring the bodywork styled by Italian designer Ghia and German coachbuilder Karmann. Soon after its introduction in 1955, the production of Karmann Ghia doubled. It has then become the car most imported to the United States. During the car's production life, more than 445,000 units were produced in Germany.

Volvo P1800

The Volvo P1800 is a two-door, two-seater sports car. It first became popular when it was featured on the hit television series aired from 1962-1969, 'The Saint' as the main car driven by Roger Moore. The P1800 model is Volvo's successful attempt to recover from its previous P1900 sports car which had failed miserably.

Made in the USA
Middletown, DE
21 February 2020